FINDING
GOD'S FOOTPRINTS
In the Path of Meditation

POEMS

Sylvia Wave Carberry

Library of Congress Control Number: 2004099012

ISBN: 0-9762909-0-1

Printed in the United States by
Morris Publishing
3212 East Highway 30
Kearney, NE 68847
1-800-650-7888

*I dedicate this book to Paramahansa Yogananda,
whose teachings have brought me gifts of peace, joy
and unfolding wisdom through meditation.*

*The cover design of this book was chosen because
its colors match the flagstones in the path
outside the SRF Hermitage at Encinitas
where the Master often walked.*

Acknowledgements

This work could not have been accomplished without the help of
my husband, William Carberry, and the following dear friends:
Jan Dunlop (who listened to me read), Marilena Scott (who believed
in my voice), my spiritual counselor (who believed in my strength),
Myrtice Kathryn Williams (who introduced me to the spiritual path)
Sarah Scheeper (expert typist) and Mary Wruck (executive assistant).

Table of Contents

Opening Prayers

Prayer for Self-Realization

O Great Spirit, O Great Self,
Self of sky, Self of sea,
Self of all, Self of me,
at dawn my mind bows down
before your hidden star.
Receive me.

At noon my hands reach out
to find Thine own.
At night my heart returns
to where you wait,
O Self of sky and sea,
never far, dreaming me.

Teach Us

Beloved Divine Mother,
who has become our earth, our skies,
our waters, our trees,
our animal sisters, our human brothers,
our human mothers, our families,
nurture us always
and cradle us in Thy never ending Love.
Teach us to see Thy Beauty,
teach us to feel Thy Beauty,
teach us to be Thy Beauty
wherever we go.

Today

O Father, I have learned
that when I've turned and returned
my words to Thee,
forming them into new patterns,
Your heart has warmed
to my praying
as I ought–
not high to Thy heavens,
but near here in my thought.

And so today I pray:
        "Indwelling Spirit,
        Infinite Child
        Divine Father, Mother Divine,
        Friend of all Friends,
        Beloved Playmate,
        teach me the Love that never ends
        begins in me."

Prayer of Thanksgiving

O Thou Mother of all conscious things,
Thy mind received my prayer.
I felt the brush of angel wings
passing through my hair.

Consciously I called to Thee:
"Save my grandchild from fear!"
"It will be done. Do not despair."
Thy words came,
oh so dear.

I felt a light all 'round my brow.
My eyes became the sun.
I saw the land beyond my dreams,
where sorrows dare not come.

I heard the song of ringing gongs,
as well as fall of water,
and standing on shores of ancient seas,
remembered I'm your daughter.

O Thou Mother of all who love,
Thou hast remembered me.

Query

Friend of all Friends, Friend Divine,
seated in the hearts of all,
are You friend of mine,
if I should fall?

Will You hear my call
as I struggle back on balance?
Friend of all,
are you a friend of mine?

O Friend Divine, O Friend of mine,
The deepest wish of my heart
is to befriend Thee
who dwellest here with me,
so near, so dear.

I'd gladly bring You flowers…
I'll listen for Your whispers,
remembering Your guidance, safe in books.
Walking hand-in-hand with Thee,
I smile Thy light on all
and You shine bright in me.

O Friend of mine,
hold me not to fall!
Help me give my all for Thee and Thine,
'til I become, like Thee,
a friend of all friends.

To Find Him

I dare not swim
where my Beloved hides
in the deep pool of my joy.

For when I dive through
into the opal-blue,
I feel His hands caressing me,
by their touching, blessing me.

In every water molecule,
He resides.
His water-arms carry me.
His love abides,
waiting for me to come and play,
to come and stay,
to bring my body, mind and soul
and dive into His consciousness
to find my meditation-body that is His.

For the Family

Our Pattern

If I extend the fingers of my love
for you to place your ring
here on my hand,
and promise I will be your love forever,
will we stand steady on this shifting sand?
Like trees whose roots are intertwined,
like dolphins swimming side by side
however deep the sea?

If we extend the fingers of our love,
to cat, to dog,
to you and you and you,
until our star-selves form into a circle,
close in thought, with stories intertwined,
we will receive the answer to
our deeper longing questions,
hiding in the pure bright thoughts
that flow into our minds.

For Thou hast grown us up
from separate, sad and lonely children,
to form a pattern of Thy Love and Song.

For My Husband

I am a hummingbird spirit,
whirring in joy.
You are the tree I live in:
towering Eucalyptus
supporting the sky,
my child's tree-mountain.

Hunting for beauty,
I see your eyes
and dive down into your heart.
Searching and thirsty,
I touch your flowers,
and sip the nectar of love.
Exhausted by flight,
I can light in your arms,
rest on your knees.

Clouded by sadness,
I can hide in your hands,
under your face,
weeping, yet safe.

Your understanding is my trunk,
my strength.
Your friendship is my branches,
my house,
the place I live in.

Your laughing leaves twinkle
around me,
wherever I look,
wherever I go.

You are my world.

Dream of Union

O to be in Santa Fe
where the sky's as blue
as the turquoise eagle
that swings around my throat.
O to sing to deserts.
filling up their space
with songs to my Beloved
of how to feel Her grace.

Here I can remember
how my soul can float
up beyond the cloud-dust,
out to meet space stark.
Here I'm ever joyful.
Here I hit my note,
making divine music,
pushing back the dark.

I want you to come with me!
Here, I'll take your hand.
Come, let's run together
just as we had planned.
Blue bowl of sky comes down to earth
around us on all sides.
Here we can be happy.
Here I'll never cry.
We'll play in red and yellow sands.
We'll run behind the wind.
We'll dance atop the sacred rock.
Our song will never end.

Sun Is the Star

Deep in the high dark midnight dome,
cold stars blaze down upon me.
Sun is the star I'm calling home,
the only light to warm me.

In your birthland of arctic night,
trees freeze as ice jewels.
The only light I want to see
is sunlight to warm me.

I sit up late by candle flame.
I write the passing hours.
Your face arises and your name.
I'm frightened of your powers.

The power to dash my stars to earth,
to break my dreams in half,
when you forget your visit's worth,
then turn on me in wrath.

Stolen hours, stolen years;
they were yours to borrow.
You are my son, the only one
whose light can banish sorrow.

(After seven years' silence, he sent a manuscript.)

Like New Lenses

When I stepped out
into the afternoon,
nothing looked the same.
As if the universe had tilted
on its axis,
sunlight splintered upward.
Branches high against the sky
wove fantastic tapestries,
matching walls in my soul's
secret room.

Blake Garden's paths
curved in impossible directions.
There was no choice
but to go on,
eyes skating off-balance
through slick transparent domes
after reading my son's bright poems.

For My Son

This is a poem for my son, Del,
who works beside the raining waters
of Puget Sound, ringed by
snow-capped peaks.

I am so proud of you, my love.
You've landed a job in the field you belong in,
passing on writing by who you are.

I hear the flaxen-haired child of three
dictating new tales of <u>The Three Musketeers.</u>
I see him crowned by a coonskin-cap,
playing at Daniel Boone.
Later at Yellow Brick Road,
after school you co-authored stories:
<u>The Adventures of Bobby Wonder,</u>
boy-detective of Richmond.

Farther back in days you don't remember,
I cuddled your silky baby-body,
while you hummed: "oly, oly, oly…"
lulling yourself to sleep.
You were my miracle, the center of my life.
You always came first with me.
No doubt I have hurt you dozens of times
in unremembered ways.
I would gladly welcome pain
if that could undo them.

And yet we are both still here
hidden inside our adulthood forms:
the ten-month old laughing child, releasing our steadying hands,
to solo across the kitchen carrying an orange.
His black-haired mother brushing back trembling waves,
in order to stay her hand –
while guarding each step with her eyes
on that snowed-in Christmas in Fairbanks.

I am so proud of you my love.

For Alice At Eighty-Eight

This is a poem to my mother, Alice,
who was my queen as a child.
I lived at her beck and call.
Faithful servant and rebel princess
were roles in my repertoire.

Now she is frail and pale and thin,
her neck terraced with many chins.
The flesh has melted from her hands.
I see veins and tendons
through cellophane skin.

I remember your sepia portrait, age twelve,
dark-eyed innocent Alice.
And a rose-tinted one from your twenties,
perfect chignon, perfect face.
You stayed young after middle-age,
appearing as forty at sixty.
After publishing stories for children,
you tried your hand at romance.

Now when I stop by to see you for lunch,
I offer you bites of ice cream.
Then I read you a story.
You enjoy my voice and the pictures,
until you lose focus –

Your worn face smiles as sweetly at me
as you would for any photo.
"What would I do without you?"
you say, eyes bright.
And I remember
you are the one who first taught me to write.

Turning Thirteen

As you step on through the curtains
of the child you used to be
onto the stage of womanhood,
and the play about to begin,
remember you are loved.

Encircled by friends and family
you glow like a golden rosebud
beginning to unfold
out to its fullest self.

In this time of transformation,
some nights you may stare in your mirror
at new spots or raggedy curls.
Remember you are beautiful,
shining from within.

Cultivating friendships,
sometime you may be asked
to do a thing you know is hurtful,
to yourself or someone else.
Remember you are wise,
and cling to what you know inside of you
is right and true.

When everyone's wound up and wild,
you can be the most sought one
if you are calm,
a center for the storm.
Remember you are brave.

As your body grows and changes,
as your mind unfolds its petals,
as the whirling dance of teenhood
grabs your hand for a pirouette,
never doubt that you are good,
beautiful and wise,
always under the eyes
of the Light that never goes out.

Feeling God's tender glance
from the sky, or the eye of a friend,
you see nothing is left to chance,
and as you begin the dance,
you easily remember you are loved.

Poem For Joan
(Turning 80)

When I think of you
I think of waves of light
dancing on rippling waters.

When I think of you
I think of holding hands,
and homemade apple strudel.

When I think of you
my mind fills with bright thoughts:
hope, courage, friendship,
striving for truth and light.

Your presence brings me joy.
Your smile wraps me in
thoughtfulness.
Your words are always kind.

When we laugh together
I hear an echo beyond our voices:
a gentle Divine giggle,
celebrating with us today.

Happy Birthday!!

Dark Song for a Daughter-In-Law

Because there is a pain here in my heart,
because of this I sometimes choose the dark.
Because I cannot meet you, daughter fair,
nor see your sky blue eyes,
nor touch your moonlight hair,
because of this I hurt.

Because I took you deep inside my soul
and welcomed you, my daughter long foretold,
and cherished you while seasons went their way,
is why tonight it is so hard to pray.

Where are you, daughter?
In what strange shadow-land does your mind roam?
And how long will you be in coming home?
I wish I could send all my hopes to you,
flying fast, to circle 'round your head,
wreathing all your mind in silver light.
Alighting by your ear,
whispering so near, "It is all right.
When you say the word, all hurts will be forgiven,
every loss replaced by hands of heaven,
gently trembling there.
All will be returned, you fancied gone,
when your soul comes home."

I miss you, daughter.

Embraced

When an isolated wave
can't feel the sea it's made of,
if it finds a friend-wave,
both in motion,
in skins of rolling molecules,
in bones of circling atoms,
they'll dance until their trembling love
becomes an arm of ocean.

Dust Angels

I love being Granny
and swoop around the house,
tidying up the dust–
for he'll be here tonight.
My strong love muscles are scrawny in my back.
Vacuuming's a Herculean task.
My mind asks, "Why?"
"For love," I tell it.
"I'm dong this for love."
Sweet grandson's coming soon.
He'll be dreaming by the moon.
All surfaces are bright,
shining stars of love
back on his sleeping face.
He must be embraced.
His mother isn't here.
And who knows if she's stopping never.
Who cares the cost!
He is not lost,
nor left alone.
Family means forever:
a patchwork quilt all glowing,
and children calmly knowing
we are here.

Her Song

Alone in the house
by myself, I
coil up and cover my head,
but I can't shut out their voices.

Depression says, "Keep quiet!
No one will understand.
These thoughts verge off the edge
of sanity.
They twist and turn around themselves
into knots of doubt,
coiling tighter and tighter
until they are
a dense metallic ring,
walling you in."

Disguise says, "I only speak
of other trivial things I've done,
or ask about you.
But the real me stays hidden
far back in a shadowy corner
of the conversation."

Delay says, "First straighten the room;
now check your calendar.
Oh, see what time it is, before you lift the phone.
Remember, you are alone."

But the Artist remembers
the Great Horned Owl
sleeping silently
on a bare limb above her,
dreaming.
At sunset he dives on his prey.
She had almost forgotten how
tight coiled metal
springs out
into flight.

And Daring knows that if she pierces
herself out through the invisible glass cage
there is a chance
she can shatter silence
into echoes.
If that happens, you'll bounce me back
a present from my past.
A long imprisoned tear-drop,
or some furry twisted creature
crouched in pain.
If an echo flows
she knows
she is not alone.

Clarity calls up the image of
a black-and-white butterfly floating,
supported on warm earth currents,
above bright grass, between pines.

He circles in a dance
that by some miracle,
keeps on flowing around me,
again and again, over and over.
He maps me as his center
for an eternity ten minutes long.
As I watch Nature weave me into Her dance,
I begin to sing Her song.

Reflections

(For Sydney at Two)

I see dancing eyes
and your curly head thrown back.
Such exuberance!
Your mischievous mouth forms new-made words
with funny meanings:
"Wait-a-second! Absolutely!"
By your baby magic, you make me new,
no longer me-alone, but me-for-you.
Here, I'm Sydney's Nanny.

As I smile with your delight,
you see me seeing you.
Here you are creating yourself,
reflected in my sight.

As you reach out to me across the table,
I seem to see myself.
I hear my tones and phrases
arrive across the bridge of years between us.

Was I like you at two? Did I giggle and wiggle
when she tried to feed me? Did she laugh too?
My Nanny, my sweet black Gale,
who patiently lingers in my soul
just behind the mirror of memory.

Which parts of me were made
when she was seeing me?

She Is the Song, I Am the Music

As I soothe my child to sleep
those notes She taught me
long ago
come floating
through my heart.

Softly I begin to sing
and in the silence
of the night
become Her instrument
again.

Invitation

You walk in high-heeled boots,
your black hair shimmering,
along dark roads you walk,
looking for a love.

　　But what you're looking for is not out there.

You walk in lacy black
through crowded streets of life,
desperate for a love,
a reason for your life.

Your eyes reflect the sky,
its purity of blue.
You've promised to be true,
when once you've found him.

　　But what you're looking for is not out there.

The boys along the way
turn to watch you pass.
Pale purity in black
casts sparks around them.

They see you as a queen,
a treasure to possess.
They cannot know your mind.
They cannot know your heart.
The wounded child inside,
the one too hurt to cry,
who cannot say goodbye–
It's she who's searching.

　　But what she's looking for is not out there.

She only knows her pangs,
her hunger to be loved
and even wolfish fangs
can look like home.
She must not be alone.
"O never leave me!"

Now pale and thin and worn
by all the pain she's borne,
she's looking for a love
to save her life.

Yet I live in her heart.
"Oh my precious child,
know I love you free,
know I love you wild.
I'm speaking from your soul.
My words are spelled in gold.

Come in to find me."

Heartfelt Question

If I extend the fingers of my love,
to touch a child and name him for my heart,
and wind his brow with countless rainbow ribbons
of bedtime stories,
and wrap his heart in soft chiffon
by fountainings of givings–
what will he offer back?
Does love grow love?

Who

My body, my puppet,
my mask, my mirror,
where shall I take you today?

Up through the forest,
out into the meadow?
Your legs may be aching,
but I pull the strings.

My body, my mask,
I'm hiding behind you.
No one can see me in here.

I thank you for cover,
a way to stay hidden
until I am ready to play.

My body, my mirror,
looking back at me,
how shall I dress you today?

In orange on a grey day,
in white on a blue day,
in leopard skirt for the long night.

Through your eyes I look outside,
but my eye looks inside.
Closed eyes are a mirror, I find.

With strong concentration,
and abandoned impatience,
I gaze in that mirror to find:

lights of gold and of blue
with flashes of silver–
revealing myself
who travels in you.

Autumn Woman

Autumn comes like a woman
wearing gold and brown.
How can she stand so still
while all her leaves are falling,
falling, falling?
Or does she throw them down?

What are these leaves to her?
Leave takings? Leavings?
Useless now, ripe to fall,
these are her past days
and her days to come.
Hearth-fires shared, childless prayers,
all she lets fall down.

Naked she stands now,
bare-branched in the present,
stretching up to touch the sky again,
after so long covered.
How is it for her, watching her leaves fall,
fly, swirling, dancing,
spinning, humming? Does it hurt?

Shivering now, she starts to dance.
Less thinking, more moving!
Laugh and sweat, forget, forget!

This woman becomes Autumn.
She's grown by loving,
deepened, ripened, turned to golden,
bearing sorrows, bearing joys,
baring her trunk to the children.

The Reverse

Who is this bronzed stranger
whose dark hair swings as she nods?
Wearing moss-green, she appears to be a foreigner,
speaking in rushes.

The force of her smile squeezes shut her eyes
when her spirit pours into words.
She is beautiful and strong.
People listen when she speaks.

This woman seems familiar,
reminds me of someone I know.
But this is the first time I've seen her,
heard her, watched her move.
She is my reverse.

Others saw her from outside:
her colors, her rhythm, her song,
bright flashes of energy
painting fireworks across thin air.

It was only I who saw her lack,
until last night, when they played the video back.

Birthday Song

Today I'm free, free to be me!
Free to sing and play all day,
to sing to Thee.
Thee and me, dancing rainbows
through the grass barefooted.

Today I'll see who we'll be –
Lions basking in the sun?
Spotted cheetahs who itch to run?
Just Thee and me today.

No more anger, no more pain.
No more drinks of that old game.
I'll be We today.
Eating scrambled eggs alone,
and a perfect scone
in the sun.
October shall be my beginning.

My Mirror

When I'm remembering Thee
You remember me;
but in truth You are
remembering Yourself.
How could I forget my Self?

In me You are so near
as to be invisible,
so close beside me
that Thy light
shining through my eyes
makes me think
it's I who see–
'though it's always Thee,
shining here in me.

You see, You think, through me.
You laugh and cry for me.
You are all my "I"s,
forever and always.

When I look at Thee,
Thou dost look at me.
I am Thy mirror;
or art Thou my mirror?
A mirror shining brightly
for me to see only Thee.

Only Thee in me.

My Body

My body, the dancer
who whirls me through life,
whose is the music
driving your steps?

And who is in charge?
It's mind that creates you,
whirling energy,
bending and turning.
You're electrons and protons
circling each other,
while between them, all glowing,
a vast sea of light,
the playing field of all life.

You're spinning to falling,
rebalancing upright,
taking deep breaths
to remember the sea.

To the music of pain,
you falter and slow.
To the music of will,
you rise and go on.
To the music of love,
you embrace those around you.
To the music of joy,
you sing as you spin.
To the music of life
you move swiftly or slowly,
or feeling the aching
of work's repetitions,

you sink down to rest–
but then hear:
  the softest song humming
  inside your right ear
  like a lullaby sung to a child.
In your mind, up you leap,
shining and wild.
You're a five-pointed star,
dancing surrounded,
upheld and restrengthened
by the infinite star-song
of Home.

Myself in Yourself

Sometimes when I close my eyes
to talk to You up close,
You pull me in, and then I'm out –
balancing a-tiptoe at the edges of myself.
Breathless, I feel dizzy,
but I could never fall.
Out here where we're face to face,
You hold me in your All.

For the Wild Ones

Spirit Sister

She stands completely still,
an ochre shadow up there on the hill,
silent, watching, soft ears spread out listening:
who is there?

A pair of butterflies rise and fall in unison
fluttering yellow and black in jagged spirals:
swallowtails dancing.

She turns her head my way.
Her wild eyes mirror my outlines
where I sit writing atop the ancient rock,
far down here.

I breathe. She sees, then looks away
and steps off lightly
across the hillside's live-oak leaves,
threading her way through flies
that hang as if suspended
on threads tied to the sky.

Nose lowered, nibbling wildflowers she goes,
not minding I've witnessed her dining,
gasped at pure wildness shining
up there on the hill:
Spirit Sister, the deer.

Caged Remembering

Four wild parrots fly
squawking as they wheel
across the winter sky.
I'd forgotten that high reel.

Bright green parrots flame
flashing through the cold
outside my windowpane.
In here I've gotten old.

Leaning onto pain,
noticing the rain,
I walk in feathered coat
among the seeds and rocks,
jungle flowers forgotten
like childhood chickenpox.

Until four chartreuse birds
coax words from my throat.
My finely patterned wing
trembles as I sing.

Whale Mind

Black and white whales know how
to leap and flash their power
around the small tank.
They live unbroken
even inside
cement walls.

When the show is over,
I dive into the aqua pool
and swim among them.
When they slow,
I mount,
for a drenching, rolling ride.
Deep inklings of their wildness
shiver up my spine.
Their spirit flashes through me:
I remember, far back in my mind,
what in me is wild
and Divine.

A Touch of Blue

As he struggled in green waters, deep and cold,
she swam by. Her hand submerged to lift him out.
He vibrated on her wrist – a huge blue dragonfly.
One by one he raised his wings, then laid them down.
None were torn. But his tiny feet clung to her skin.
"I'll swim you in." She placed him gently in her hair.

Praying for safe passage, she breast-stroked to the beach,
holding her head like a flower.
At the reeds she bent to dislodge that blue rider.
Was he even there? Then she felt his tickling legs
as he stepped from hair to fingers,
toward sand, she thought. But suddenly a buzzing whirr!
She craned her neck in time to see
him turning small against blue sky,
saved, alive and free!
And she knelt in joy to Thee.

To Love a Dog

To Love a Dog

To love a dog is to open a door
to a magnifying view,
to open a door that leads into a forest,
a forest of poem-trees stretching their branches,
of never-thought thinkings waving at you,
as far as your mind can see.

But the inner eye sees deeper still,
to the Heart of the Light of the World.
And in that Heart is the heart of a dog,
surrounding your heart with her own.

Surrounding your frown with her wolfy smile,
surrounding your hands in a cloud of her fur,
lashing your knees with her plume-style tail,
prancing in front and behind.

No use to hang back–let her bring you out!
Dance with her, no matter the pain!
For there is no light like the love that she gives.
Give that cosmic smile its way.

To love a dog is to close the door
on smallness and worrying pain
and step on out in the forest of God,
of laughter and running and rain,
the home you come back to again and again
when you open yourself to a dog.

Love's Reply

This is a poem for Wolfy-Baby,
the dog I longed for a thousand times
as a child, but never found,
whose almond eyes look back to see me
from far ahead on the trail.

Bright fringe lights your outline
against dark hills.
You're black over sand-tones
with silver shadows,
pale tail curled like an ostrich feather,
silk ears flapping wild.

No more long nights on hard pavement for you,
ears filled with harsh big rigs' zooms.
No more dark days behind closed doors for me,
nor bleak thoughts in empty rooms.

Driving on empty, I pulled to a stop.
As I turned, there you were,
chin on paws, eyes alert,
sent by the Friend Divine.

Now I'm never alone in my house,
and when we go out,
home-energy stretches between us,
an invisible life-line.
Your path never darts toward the distance,
but holds me in multiple circles,
ever returning.
You watch me so as not to lose me,
as I watch you.

(At a graduation of Canine Companions for Independence)

The Golden Times

Golden energy filled the room.
Humans filled the pews
at the Luther Burbank Center,
humans young and old,
and between them, dotted here and there,
silent golden dogs,

well-trained dogs with large brown eyes
and gentle noses. All the golden necks
wore emblem scarves of blue.

Magic was about to happen,
that ancient bond of kinship reaffirmed,
the golden strands of friendship
beginning to be braided
between disparate beings.

A puppy-trainer led a golden retriever
onto the stage, and handed the leash
to Claire, who's nine.
All around her wheelchair,
golden light did shine.

Anna, whose ears are challenged,
received her wagging hearing-dog
with radiant golden smiles.

Later in the lobby, humans nibbled cookies,
while at their feet, secure on long blue leashes,
silent friendly noses touched
or pressed the floor for crumbs.

While everywhere throughout the air
golden waves shimmered joyously,
because the hearts of humans
had expanded out
to hold the ocean of God's Love
shining through His dogs.

Bright Promise

When moonbeams cast their shadows,
bright and dark the night,
your image darts from corners
barely out of sight.

You've been my life's companion,
full of charming wiles,
on parkland trails or city streets,
you followed me for miles.

This year I saw you slowing,
felt the end in sight.
But since it came, I'm not the same.
With you I sent my light.

O beloved canine,
how can I let you go,
unless I see that you and I
are more than what I know.

More than dog and human,
what we are is souls,
bonded by our friendship
however long time rolls.

So my shining soul-dog,
my ever faithful friend,
we must never doubt it:
we will meet again.

Writing for Play

A Lesson In Writing

Writing remembers
how to be with myself in peace
instead of alone,
my inner child nurtured
by the hands of the Eternal Mother.

Writing remembers
that beauty must not by forgotten.
The good, the bad and the ugly
were certainly present.
But writing heals the past.

Writing remembers
events never seen before
and creates a new world
of joy and sharing.

Writing remembers
a secret language from childhood
and draws out love
from the heart of the universe.

At the Himalayan Fair in Berkeley

Sitting under the oak trees,
together, you and I,
hearing children squabbling,
but we can hold our peace.
Stretched out on a blanket
woven in Mexico,
we're dreaming Himalayas
and shadows on the snow.
Shadows framing brightness,
lighting up the dark.
You and I are quiet
for you hold my heart.
Tell me where we're going,
up along the rim?
Up to touch the Sky Gods,
where we'll dance with Him.

Heights

There are many pathways up
the mountainsides of life,
but the one I love to follow most
is the trail that leads to ice,

to icy boulders in the sun,
to pinnacles of ice and snow:
the laughter of Parvati rings
across the shining deeps.

I'll climb the Himalayas high
until my breath is breathing sky,
until my feet touch powder white
along the rim of world.

There I'll sit laughing on the peak
that few have dared to reach,
knowing the joy of goal achieved,
with no doubts left to breech.

Faces

Golden faces, tan-gold faces, brown faces,
dark-brown faces, red faces,
black faces, white faces too.
All these mask You,
O Spirit, the One
who hides behind us all.

A woman in Tibet holds a prayer wheel.
She spins written chants to Chenrezi.
Unvoiced, still He hears her.
He, the all-seeing One,
the all-holding One.
He is You, holding us all.
You laugh with us,
You cry with us;
You see us beautiful,
and know we are very smart.
You believe we can follow the path home,
although it is winding and long
and steep and narrow.
You're sure we'll make it quite soon.
Because of course You remember
that only this morning we set out,
calling back, "I'll go play now,"
and turned our rainbowed faces down toward earth,
while Your Hand spun the prayer wheel.

An Answer to Wallace Stevens

The palm at the end of the mind,
once so pale and indistinct,
hums in the wind when I come.

I settle down in the golden sand,
pushing up hills with my curling toes,
turn on my back to see:

high fronds like fingers
tickling sky keys,
while above and beneath,
within and without,
trembles thunder
from the Sea.

(At the Vietnam Memorial Wall)

Reflections on Marble

My fingers slide along
shiny black marble.
Leaning closer,
to look for his name,
I see my face,
my nose and hair.

At first I'm on the surface –
my fingerprints obscuring
carven words, and
dim reflections.

Then the stone takes me in.
I am where he is –
on a shining astral planet.
Dreams of wars forgotten,
in joy we dance again.

Song for the Goddess

Eating in silence, I am feeding
myself as a baby –"how about this?
A little of this, dear?"
I am both child and mother,
a fusion, a transfusion…
metamorphosis:
baby to child
to emerging woman,
becoming snake, becoming Goddess.
Venus rising from the waves,
diving through the waves,
brave and afraid,
laughing and shaking.
But her core is
fire in the dark,
a vibrant candle-flame
creating shadows, creating my light.

Mind and Sky

The sky is a white blanket
draped over the trees
as the air bursts like a pillow.
Wild water-feathers lash my face,
arrow through my hair.

In my mind despair
is wrestling with peace,
twisting itself like a snake writhing.
But peace stays golden cool,
a mountain lake so long serene
it cannot be troubled
by even a hundred-headed snake.

The sky is a blue blanket
folded at my feet,
as I swim the glass surface
over the depths
of my ancient golden mind.

Wild Yoga

There's an eagle soaring eastward
to find my home afar,
beyond the seas of silence,
beyond the last pale star.
He flies to the sound of music
to the drumbeat of my heart,
and his eye is fixed on the present,
and his wingbeats draw the chart:
the chart across mental breakers,
the map over sorrowing seas,
to a pinnacle of quiet
where samadhi waits for me.
I'll climb up jagged footholds,
I'll grasp at spiky shards,
to reach high concentration
beyond pale flickering stars.
When I get there he'll be waiting,
my eagle of yogic strides,
to welcome me home to his eyrie
on the inner mountainside.
Together we'll call Saraswati,
the goddess who answers prayer.
In response to our wild worship,
quite soon She'll touch us there.

New

I've learned a new way to live:
my life has become the poem.
The thoughts I'm thinking,
I've never thought before.
I feel like a child who has found a lost friend
in such an unlikely place:
Tenth and Heinz, downtown Berkeley
at such an unlikely hour:
1:30 to 1:45 every workday.

An author said that when the ego contacts the soul,
there's flirting at first.
Then comes irresistible attraction
and longing for communion.

Communion begins listening to him,
hearing his trust,
my heart touched like when a lost black kitten
crept onto my lap long ago.

Communion begins talking to him,
sharing my sorrow and pain
sometimes; then watching
his many dear efforts to stay with me
in spite of all that.
He has the gift of true compassion,
and doesn't even know it!

Our life is a poem in process of being written,
day by day, minute by minute,
as we share the feeling of faith
and compare small miracles.

And so even though at times I feel old,
I won't scold myself anymore
for living a poem.
For God is friendship.

For Healing

Who You Are

You are a rare wild orchid, magically lit from within,
but warmed outside by flaming sun of passion.
You are strong, and cling tenaciously to love.
No jungle predator can tear you from your home,
for you protect your own.
But when shrieking storms have blown down
all the stable trunks of home,
and you stand swaying in the shifting wind,
know this, my friend:
you are more than who you think.
No one can define you, or diminish you,
even at the brink of loss and sorrow.
You fold within yourself
seeds of growth and power,
the light of understanding.
These contain the blueprint of your larger family.

Song of Celebration

Father, Mother, Friend, Beloved God,
I want to dance in the sky,
I want to run on the ocean.
Hear me sing in the silence
until You come.

I have too much joy not to share it.
I have too much pain not to bear it.
These two are my twin sisters
when I'm alone.

I'm going to dance in the moonlight,
I'm going to dance with my sisters.
We'll heal the broken circle with our song.

We'll invite You to come if You want to –
We'll call all the children to join us,
dancing in the forest,
dancing in our home.

I'm waiting for my Guru.
I'm waiting for my friend.
I have to let Him know me,
to have the courage to show me,
for I have understood
He is my own.

Dancing in the forest,
dancing in my home,
dancing in the moonlight,
dancing with my own.

Opening

Windows nailed shut,
doorways dark,
still I sing the songs of childhood.

Growth

Over the roof
of my childhood's home
rare wild roses climb.

After Sorrow

From the dark pool prayers
leap up silver
to tail-dance in red afternoon.

Hope

Purple flowering vine
grasps joy with a thousand tendrils
above sorrow's compost pile.

Thy Grace

Lying in tall grass,
blue sky
brushes my eyebrows.

Fear

Dog-walking above the quarry,
sunlit conversation
casts pit-bull shadows.

Forlorn

Tall dark Eucalyptus friend,
they cut you
from my sky.

Thirst

My eyes drank
Eucalyptus wine
through the western windows.

Invisible Scene

Outside my window,
clear space that you no longer fill
has taken form.

For Wolfy Baby

You've been our dog for a year,
but not until now, did you carry
my sock to your bed.

Under Clouds

Fluffs of fur
caught on thorny branches.
Dogless, I walk forlorn.

Pathless

Woods-walking alone,
I stumble on fallen branches.
Where is that bouncy shepherd?

Divine Lesson

When this body's aches and pains
try to touch my mind,
I remember who I am.

You have taught me this:
I am a spark of the Infinite.
I am your child divine.

And 'though I've dreamed
that I was ill,
I have faith I will wake
in the arms of joy
listening to Your Song
of shining healing.

Have You Heard

Have you heard these ancient words of comfort?

Each time the Mother Divine reaches out
to touch you tenderly,
Her hand creates a shadow.
Perceived as sorrow or pain,
that shadow passes through your mind,
soon before She fills your soul
with Her drenching light of joy.

Never Mind

Never mind if there are troubles!
I cannot be afraid,
because I know that You
are all in all.
I am made of the very substance
of Your Spirit,
encircled in the radiance
of Your Love.

On Beauty

The beauty of the sky
is a very high beauty –
rainbow lights,
misty floating forms,
the wide expanse of blue.
But your beauty outshines it.

The beauty of the earth
is a very deep beauty –
solid and fertile,
row on row of nature's bounty,
velvet grasses, star-flowers.
But your beauty is deeper.

The beauty of the sea
is my favorite beauty –
the rocking rhythm of her waves,
unending peace in her shining waters,
the sound at her shores.
The sea is my mother
and I worship her beauty.
But your beauty captures my heart.

The beauty you are is the beauty of meeting –
two streams coming together,
merging, mingling, dancing, laughing,
touching each other on every level;
brave enough to mingle;
strong enough to know our
individuality will not be weakened,
but strengthened by our meeting.

Let's be silver sprites
dancing in the forest –
sometimes Thou and I
but now a ring of moonlight,
now a faraway birdsong,
now a shiver of joy.

Stories from Home

Holy Star

And Thou, my lost great gentle star
dost still encircle me.
Thy glimmerings slip between the pages of my mind,
illuminating pure thoughts, pushing back the dark.
Thy warmth enfolds my heart in a golden halo,
which wreaths in turn the face of the Master.
In His eyes, Thou art mirrored as twins.
His glances shoot bright arrows,
piercing my gloom.
Thy rays of pure white light reach out to me,
like hands' extended fingers –
longing for my touch
in the darkness of my sight.

Thou playest for me the music of the spheres.
I listen through the mist of nature's tears,
until most softly from the deeps of me,
I hear at last Thy voice:

"Come home, my child, come home."

"My Father, here I come!"

To Go Within

The tentacles of my mind
explore dark inner seas,
reach out to touch bright fish
of fairy fancies;
tickle sea-horse tails;
swim off among song-dolphins,
gently hunting.

Then trembling for larger prey,
those fingers finally float
in utter stillness.

It's then I'm carried away–
Breathless I ride a shining whale,
leaving a silvery vanishing trail
as we dive toward
deeps of Bliss.

Meditation

When I close my eyes to meditate,
in the darkness, there is music,
in the silence, hum of atoms,
in deeper stillness, rumbling ocean.
Do I sit alone?

Haunting wind-chime draws me inward.
Whose breath, the wind that
sets it shining,
in tones receding, calling me?
Pulling me. I must follow,
follow the song of forgotten nearness,
disguised as faraway.

When broken silence doesn't matter,
I am there. Or You are here.
Somehow my center has been shifted
from small point of effort
to far-spreading Being,

filled with Thy waters
and spilling out further,
'til I know I belong
to Thy vastness:
the Sea is me.

Her Touch

The sea was flecked with silver,
the trees were flecked with gold.
Beneath the Eucalyptus,
I felt my soul unfold.
And stretching out my wings then,
ready to fly bold,
I felt my Divine Mother
touch me in the wind,
breathing 'round me gently,
inviting, "Now come in."

I closed my eyes and floated
out into Her hands.
The rings upon Her fingers
sparked rainbows in my mind.
"Just stay there, I'll lift you,"
I heard Her say to me,
my being still sufficient
for gaining liberty.

"I thought I had to please You,
that I must long be good."

"No, my child, your love is wild,
but I have understood."

My Soul Stays in Santa Fe

Turquoise eagle
carried home
reminds me
freeway's end
is no longer home.
My soul stays in Santa Fe.

She plays deep in canyons
around adobe rocks
along a turquoise river.

Pueblo dust blows
above the cliffs
over pink rocks
gold rocks
orange rocks.
Empty desert full.

I'll sit in the shade
of this ancient cottonwood,
six armspans circle her,
breathing peace,
dreaming.

My soul stays in Santa Fe.

Mystic Conversation

You heal me, Mother, when I sit
in your midst on dry redwood sprigs,
and above my hair is Your leafy hair,
and behind my back sound Your chords of harmony,
as high silent trees in threes and fours.

I feel You, Mother, in the soft breeze
that stirs around my face,
and in the sunlight's rainbow kiss
upon my lashes.
I hear You sing in the continual stream
of falling water, and see Your face
reflected in green ponds
and fronds and ferns.

Here I cannot pretend to be alone.
In plain sight You stand all around me,
wrapped in flowers and lacy ferns.
Your mantle of cellophane green
filters Love's light into me.

You keep saying, "Two.
You and I, alive together,
this day and forever, dearest one."

Shanti

It was quiet in the chapel
where nine sat still as statues,
reaching out with minds and hearts
toward Thee.

It was even more than quiet,
the silence thick and silvery.
I sat and leaned against it,
held in airy arms.

Thy calmness smoothed my forehead,
brushed my brows and eyelids,
then with a sigh it gently
hushed my breath.

Now we were two no longer,
but nested in each other
like Russian lacquer boxes,
melted in each other
like wax into the candle,
and shining with the searless
flame of love.

And tender in the chapel,
Peace knew eleven sat,
meditating heart to heart
as One.

Her Blessing

I told Her I was hungry,
an apple would suffice.
She sent to me an apple tree,
and in its arms She rocked me
and fanned me with perfume,
over my head a canopy
of fragrant lacy bloom.
And the fruit She fed me,
its flavor I cannot tell.

I told Her I was thirsty,
that fruit juice would be nice.
She sent to me the wine of love
in the chalice of my heart.
I sip it when I think of you
whenever we're apart.

I told Her I was starving –
for warm words, a caressing glance.
She must have stopped Her housework
among the stars and suns,
just turned and only thought of me
to do the thing She's done.

She said, "Here is my magic veil
woven of healing love.
Would you want to wear it?"
And She wrapped me in its folds.
Then I felt your arms around me
and the strength you gave to me
rebuilt the broken circle of my love.
And when I looked into your eyes,
peering deeply in, seeking you –
out shone Her star eternal
from behind the veil,
shining through.

I had asked Her for a remedy
to heal my aching heart,
just something small,
a balm, perhaps,
a healing herb, perchance.
But when She heard my longing,
and when I felt Her heart,
Her answer was not quiet
or just a thing apart,

but churning whirling currents
in torrents She poured out,
until I floated in Her Love
within me and without.

Alone no more,
I saw She came Herself,
disguised as you.

What Is Peace?

Peace is the wordless hum of singing silence
filling the space inside me after prayer.
It transforms from inner to outer
in the blink between breaths.
It is magical–quivering like a dragonfly
drying wet wings in the sun–
shining like sunlight through a prism,
rainbowing my world.

Peace fills the space around me
like furry snow,
becoming radiant light,
larger than my body,
wider than my mind.
Peace expands me out until
I fill the room,
then billow through the sky.

Or I can pull it close–
and wrap it like a cloak around me,
softly warm, yet infinitely strong.

Peace is Divine Mother's hum of love
to all Her children,
and the gentleness
and strength I feel
when my Father holds me
in His quiet cosmic hug.

I am safe in Peace.

Peace Is Looming

Great-Grandmother Spirit,
teach us to weave ten million thoughts
and sing them in our minds,
that war may loom no more.

Great-Great-Grandmother,
teach us to weave ten hundred words
and write them in our hearts,
that we sow war no more.

Great-Great-Great-Grandmother,
make us weave deeds ten thousand strong,
and dance them holding hands.
No more wars.

Spin your necklace of stars around our necks,
so we speak in constellations
of friendship, hope, forgiveness.
We'll hum the song from your loom of peace
against the dark.

His Golden Ones

(in the Encinitas Retreat gardens)

The pond is deep, yet light can reach far down
to those who listen. Strolling under the leafy
canopy, we watch sun-rays pierce the surface
and flicker along the mossy bottom
where the golden ones feed.
Who are these glowing beings, undulating around
the curving boundaries of the pool?
They glide beneath each other softly,
pass across each other gently,
tenderly brushing fins like friends
who want to share each drop of light.
Their dance is graceful.
Peace blooms in their coming and going.
Yet we have forgotten who they are
and what their pool is made of.
As we walk around the pond,
the fish seem to follow us.
Soft airs around us shimmer,
boundaries snap and quiver,
as silence seems to swallow us.
In a flash of light the mind's sight
opens out to perceive the garden's nature:
We are the circling golden ones,
living always inside Divine Waters,
all engulfed in the deepest well
of Master's tender love.

Friendship Is God

Friendship is a love
that grows stronger forever,
in more and more places,
in more and more hearts,
spreading out to the stars.

Friendship is sharing
laughter and joy
and kinship in God
with each other forever.

Friendship is a magnetic field
between two beings
that is charged
with the Love of God.
And both share it.
And God holds them.

Friendship is having an elder brother
for whom no trouble or fault
is too heavy to hear,
too heavy to bear,
nor heavy enough
to break our friendship.

Friendship is Guru.
Guru is friendship.

Friendship carries me
safely to the port of Joy,
to the shores of Love Divine,
where I feel
I am you;
you are me.

We are so near and dear
that I stand at your side
as you,
and you are me
in my heart.

Morning Silence

Aroused by light that softly
permeates my mind,
I sit up secretly to offer You my prayer.
Thoughts that tremble in the air,
words said in the mind in silence,
reach the regions where You hear.
As I breathe in, as I breathe out,
I find the place where You are near,
smiling in my silence.

About the Author

Sylvia Wave Carberry has been writing poetry since 1981.
Her work has appeared in the following gift books:
Graces (HarperSanFrancisco), Bless the Day (Kodansha
International), Bedside Prayers (HarperSanFrancisco) and Mothers
and Daughters (Harmony Books), all edited by June Cotner.

Earlier in life she received a B.A. in English Literature from
U.C.L.A. and an M.A. in Transformative Arts from John F. Kennedy
University.

The author currently teaches creative writing at West Contra Costa
Adult Education, Richmond, California.

Ordering Information

To order additional copies of the book "Finding God's Footprints,"
please complete this form and mail it along with your payment
of $19.95 per book to the author:

    Sylvia Wave Carberry, 5920 Jordan Ave., El Cerrito, CA 94530.
    Send check or money order only. Please do not send cash.
    Sorry, credit cards cannot be accepted.
    Please allow 6-8 weeks for delivery.

Name: _____

Address: _____

_____

_____

Phone: _____

Email: _____

Number of Books ($19.95 each): _____

Total Payment: _____

—Thank you for your order.

A portion of the proceeds from the sale of this book
will be donated to the Self-Realization Fellowship/
Yogoda Satsanga Society of India.